AROUND TOWN

AIRPORT

by Adeline J. Zimmerman

TABLE OF CONTENTS

tadpole books

WORDS TO KNOW

airplanes

airport

gate

line

packed

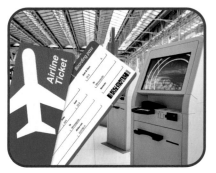

tickets

AIRPORT

Let's go to the airport!

bag

We have our bags packed.

Airline
Ticket

Boarding pass

Seat & Class
26 B

A

To Minneapolis

Remarks

Seat
26 B

Gate
A34

To Minneapolis

Airline use
054780 A

kiosk

Activate me by touching the screen

We get our tickets.

We get in line.

gate

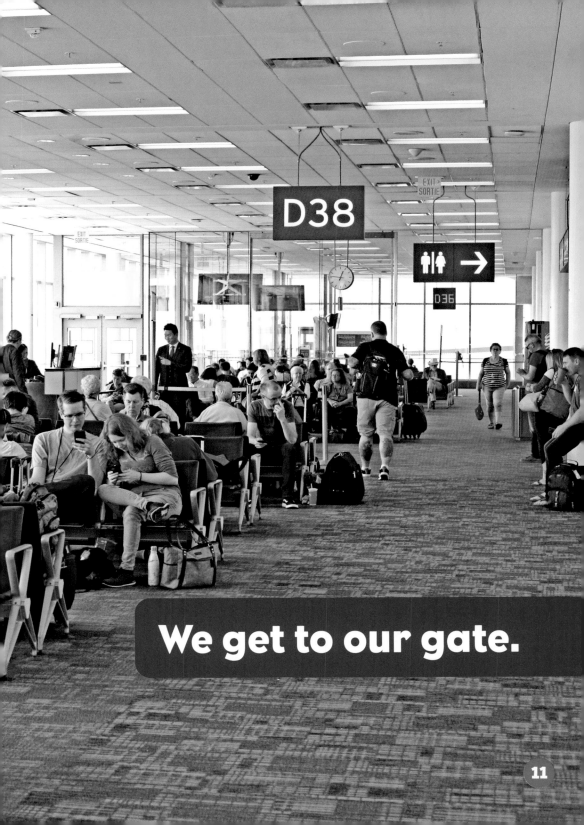

We get to our gate.

We watch the airplanes.

Ours is here!

We get on the airplane.

Let's go!

LET'S REVIEW!

What are these people doing at the airport?

INDEX